A Short History of
The Morris Family of Bishops Lydeard, Somerset

Lucy Fox

First published by Busybird Publishing 2025

Copyright © 2025 Lucy Fox

ISBN:
Print: 978-1-923501-60-7

This work is copyright. Apart from any use permitted under the *Copyright Act 1968*, no part of this publication may be reproduced, stored in a retrieval system or transmitted in any form or by any means, electronic, mechanical, photocopying, recording or otherwise, without the prior written permission of Lucy Fox.

The information in this book is based on the author's experiences and opinions. The author and publisher disclaim responsibility for any adverse consequences that may result from use of the information contained herein. Permission to use any external content has been sought by the author. Any breaches will be rectified in further editions of the book.

Cover design: Busybird Publishing

Layout and typesetting: Busybird Publishing

Busybird Publishing
2/118 Para Road
Montmorency, Victoria
Australia 3094
www.busybird.com.au

Prologue

Lucy Fox – January 2024

On 28 December, 2022 Great-Aunt Margaret, as she was known to most of us, died peacefully in her armchair at a nursing home she had recently moved to. Great-Aunt Margaret — Margaretta Gweneth Morris (formerly White) — was 93-years-old when she died. She had outlived her husband, Alan Herbert Morris, by 25 years; they had no children.

Margaretta's death unlocked a trust – the Alan Morris Trust – that benefited 14 of us; all the descendants of Alan's brother John (Jack) and his wife Lily (Judy) Morris. (Lucy and Simon Fox, Alison, Claire, Andrew and Denise McLoughlin, Katie Morris, Conrad and Sarah Guyatt, James and Matthew Shiels,

Sam Arbuthnot, Amy and Rose Morris). Charles Morris inherited Pound Farm, as he is Alan's only nephew to carry the Morris name, and as a result is not a beneficiary.

The trust triggered an urge to find out how it came about and where we all come from on this side of the family.

The following is my interpretation, from the copious amounts of documents found online as well as diaries and other documents willingly handed over to me by my Uncles John and Tom Morris.

While some relatives worked and lived in India most of the action takes place in West Somerset on the farms: East Lydeard, Pound, Portman and Conquest close to the village of Bishops Lydeard…

This is our story…

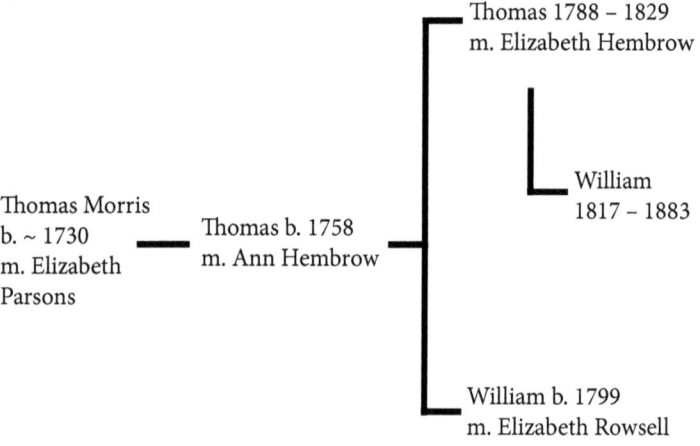

The Distant Hazy Past

While this story starts in 1817, the Morris family's started much earlier. The earliest direct ancestor I can find is a Thomas Morris born sometime in the 1730s in the hamlet named Stoke St Gregory. In 2024 it has a population of under a 1000 residents; in the 18th century it would have been far less. It's likely Thomas and his family were farmers.

The majority of farms at the time consisted of 60 acres or less, with some farmers only having ten or twelve acres. These small farms were original encroachments of Woodhill Common before Woodhill Road defined their boundaries. The Huntham farms were larger. One hundred and twenty acres in Huntham Road was farmed by Robert Barrington, and William Hembrow had 150 acres. William

Rowsell was at Huntham Farm, 160 acres. By far the largest was Slough Farm with 307 acres farmed by Thomas Hembrow[1].

The Barrington, Hembrow and Rowsell families are all a part of our story.

Thomas Morris's son with his second wife, Elizabeth Parsons, was also named Thomas and was baptised in Stoke St Gregory in January 1758. This younger Thomas married into one of the big families still living in the area – the Hembrows. Thomas and Ann Hembrow married on 4 June 1781 and she signed the register with an 'X'.

Their son, another Thomas, was born in 1788. He married Elizabeth Hembrow (possibly/probably a cousin) at Stoke St Gregory on 19 August, 1816. Sometime in the 1780s they moved to Lyng. It's believed they lived at Home Farm, now Glebe Farm, that today borders the A361.

At least one Morris stayed in Stoke St Gregory – William Morris (Thomas's much younger brother born in 1799). William Morris (presumably him) was registered as the occupant of nine of fifteen lots in an estate listed for lease in 1824.

---

1 - Stoke St Gregory History Page, www.gregorystoke.org

The Anglican Church, under the Worshipful the Dean and Chapter of Wells, was a significant landholder in the area and they were selling the leasehold of the land for 99 years. William had married into the Rowsell family – Elizabeth Rowsell – two years earlier, on 17 June, 1822 at Stoke St Gregory.

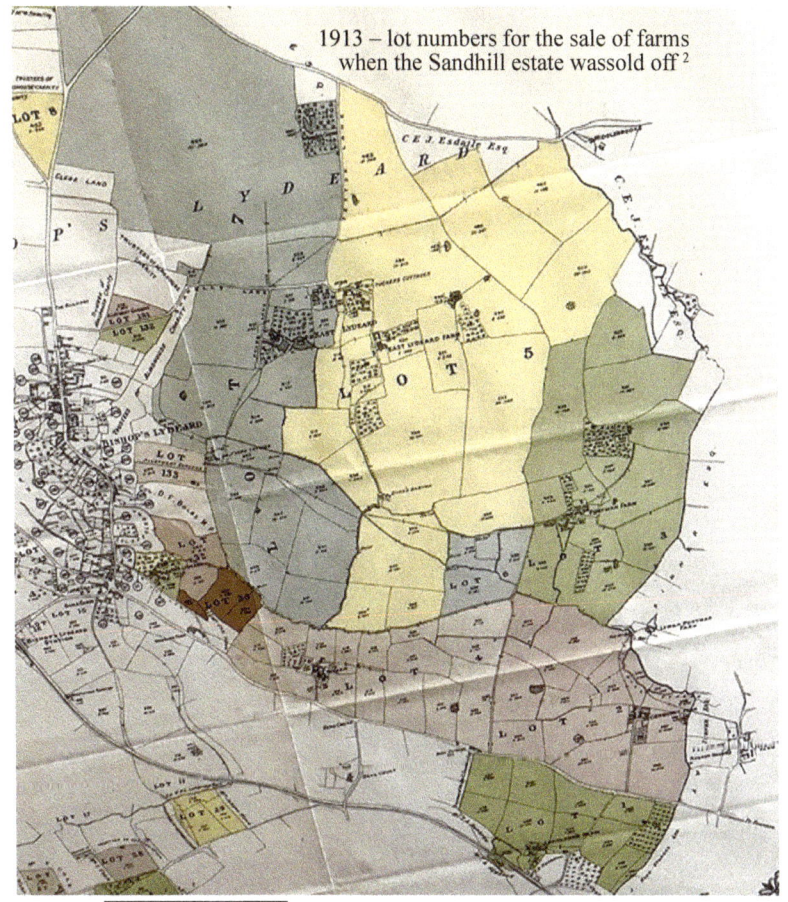

2 - Map courtesy of Thomas William Morris

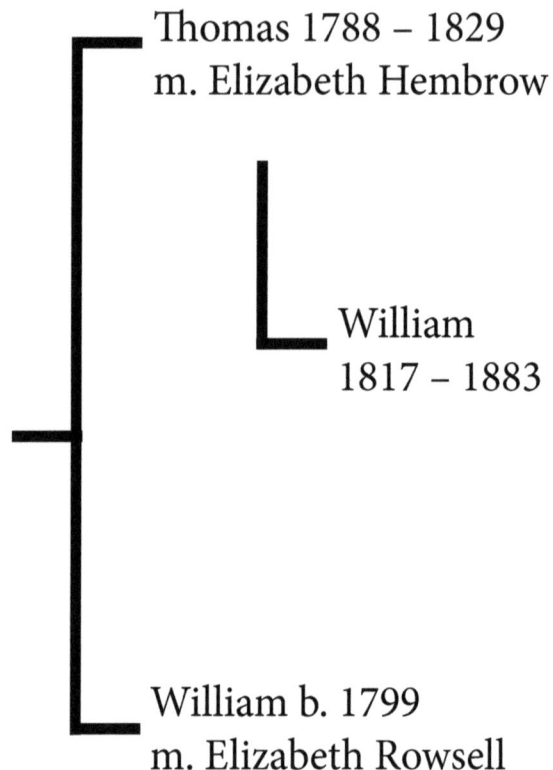

1817 – The Year This Story Really Starts

The year of William Morris's birth, 1817, was a difficult one. Two years after the end of the Napoleonic War, it followed the so-called year without summer. In 1816, the biggest volcanic eruption in 10,000 years occurred on an island in Indonesia. Mount Tamboro literally exploded, throwing huge quantities of ash so high into the atmosphere it lowered the temperature in the Northern Hemisphere for the next twelve months by over half a degree.

This lead to harvests in Europe and England being 75% less than normal. There was snow in June and July and in Ireland it rained for eight solid weeks triggering the potato famine and a mass exodus via the Western ports of England to America. In Europe people were also on the move, trying to avoid starvation, most heading East. This resulted in a typhus epidemic that killed tens of thousands.

1817 was also a bad year for literature with the death of Jane Austen at only 41.

***

What the social and economic impact of this meant for Thomas and Elizabeth (formerly Hembrow) Morris when their son William was born is hard to say – but as they were farming a distance away from towns with large populations and therefore not on a route that refugees might be travelling – it is likely they were largely unaffected.

Unusually for the period William was the only child of Thomas and Elizabeth. He was baptised at Lyng in September 1817 and it's likely the family were living at Glebe Farm.

Thomas was probably a tenant farmer as it was difficult to own land in that part of Somerset. In the early 1800s much of it was locked up in the large family estates that had existed since the 1500s; changing hands only when loyalties changed with Kings.

William was also a tenant farmer his whole adult life and was fortunate to have had some level of education, (you'll see his beautiful handwriting in his will later on). At the time a quarter of parishes in England had no school and many families could not afford to send their children anyway. He would have been working from a young age.

In 1829, when William was only 12, his father, Thomas, died. I can find no record of what or why he died but as a result of his death everything would have changed for the family. It's hard to know what happens next but William can be traced to be living in Lyng (actually West Lyng because there was West and East Lyng separated by a short stretch of road) until around 1854. But as tenant farmers I can't see how they might have remained on the farm where he was born.

Our story comes back into focus in the middle of the 1830s when a landowner becomes well and truly part of our family story. William Payne did not have a huge amount of land, but enough to place him well above the social and economic standing of a tenant farmer.

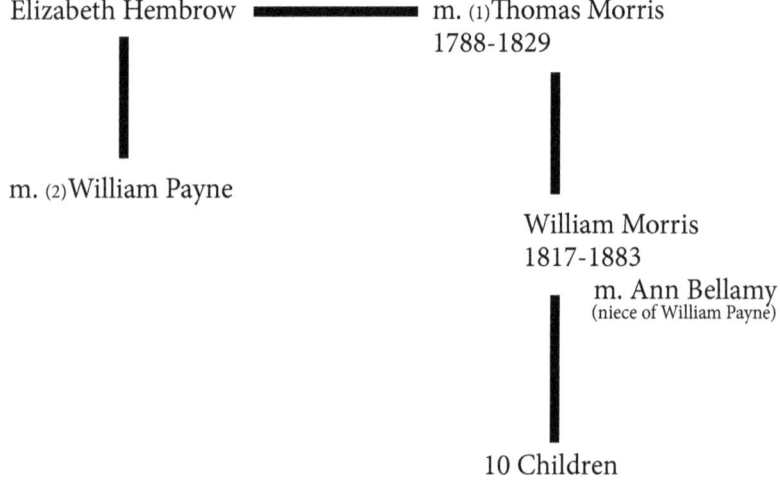

1836 – The Year of Two Weddings

On the 26 September, 1836 at St Bartholomew's Church in Lyng, William Payne marries Elizabeth Morris, William Morris's widowed mother. Exactly two weeks later on 4 October, 1836. William, aged 19, marries Ann Bellamy also at St Bartholomew's. The witnesses to their marriage were William Payne (William's new stepfather and also his wife Ann's, uncle) and Ann's sister Joanna (Joanna married Jonas Rowsell from Stoke St Gregory).

In relatively quick succession William and Ann had ten children, nine of whom were baptised at St Bartholomew's.

The Ten Children of William and Ann Morris

William Payne	born 24 Sept, 1837	baptised 30 Oct, 1837 at Lyng
Elizabeth	born 2 June, 1839	baptised 12 June, 1839 at Lyng
Thomas	born 31 March, 1841	baptised 26 April, 1841 at Lyng
Francis	born 11 June, 1843	baptised 9 July, 1843 at Lyng
Edwin	born 28 November, 1845	baptised 10 Dec, 1845 and dies 28 April, 1846 at Lyng
Emma Ann	born 4 April, 1847	baptised 3 May, 1847 at Lyng
Edwin Henry	born 10 May, 1849	baptised 15 June, 1849 at Lyng
Edward	born 18 February, 1851	baptised 24 March, 1851 at Lyng
John	born 2 March, 1853	baptised 25 March, 1853 at Lyng
Charles	born 1 March, 1855 at East Lydeard	

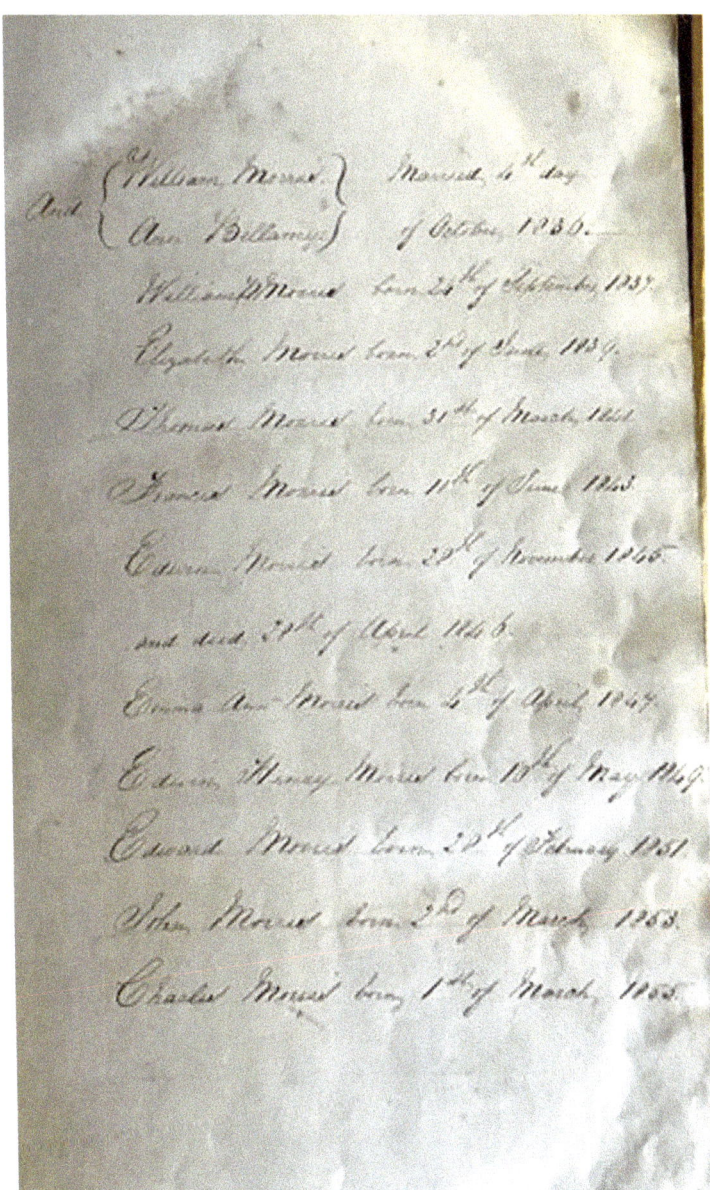

Page from family Bible at East Lydeard Farm

The 1830s were difficult times to be tenant farmers and worse still to be a farm labourer. Huge areas of land, swallowing up hundreds of small farms, were being bought by the newly rich who had made their money manufacturing or via corporations such as The East India Company. They were people who generally had no, as they said at that time, 'attachment' to the land they owned. Thousands of people who had traditionally earned their living by some form of agriculture fell into poverty.

In 1830, the year after William's father Thomas Morris died, the 'starving field labourers of the southern counties rioted in support of their demand for a wage of half-a-crown a day. Three of them were hanged and 420 were deported to Australia',[3] (which, if they survived the journey and the sentence, could have been the making of them). And heaven help you if you were caught catching a rabbit or any other form of game to feed your family or sell to survive – that was also a sentence of seven years in Australia.

---

3 - The Pelican History of England 1961

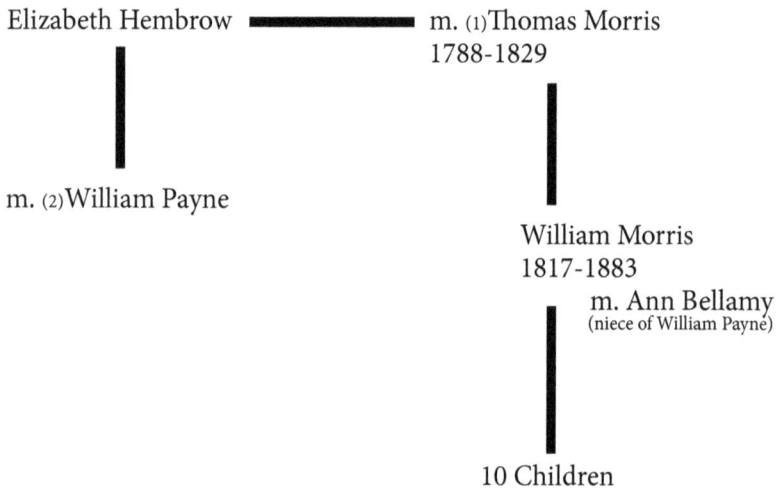

Who is William Payne and why is he in the Morris story?

William Payne was born in North Curry in 1783, and lived for some time in Lyng and Bishops Lydeard.

When Payne married Elizabeth Morris her husband Thomas had been dead for seven years. How long he had known Elizabeth and her son William is something I have not been able to find out.

The 1841 census is the first modern day census in the UK, at this time the country's population was recorded as just over 18 million people. While that first census was an incredible feat, it is remarkable for its lack of detail – no occupations are given and no specific addresses recorded. However it does record that five years after William Payne and Elizabeth married they are registered as living in Lyng. Elizabeth's son William and his wife Ann Morris are recorded living in a separate household.

In William Payne's census return he and Elizabeth are living quite comfortably – I presume on a farm because there are two males aged 20 and 15 living with them who may have been labourers. As the list of property that comes up for sale after Payne's death does not include anything in Lyng it is likely the Paynes are tenants there. That census also records that William Payne Morris, three-years-old, (William and Ann Morris's eldest child), is staying with Payne and Elizabeth.

William Morris is listed in the census as being 24-years-old and his wife, Ann, is 26 but their household is more convoluted. Their second child and eldest daughter, Elizabeth, aged two is with them and a Thomas Harrington who is listed as being only one month old. It's possible that Thomas Harrington is actually William and Ann's third child, Thomas Morris, born in April 1841. There is also Mary Brewer, aged 15, Andrew Brewer and a girl Mary Pine aged 11. It's likely therefore William Morris and his family were also farming.

William Morris may have received financial help from Payne. I base this assumption of the high level of poverty in the countryside in the 1830s and 40s and the fact that William has his own farm with employees at only 24-years-of-age. A search by Alison (Mcloughlin/Westcott) found no will for Thomas, which probably means he didn't have one – either because he died relatively young (age 41), because he died suddenly or because he really had nothing to leave – possibly all three[4].

Things become clearer in 1851 when the UK began to conduct a census every decade at the end of March/beginning of April. These censuses provide more detail. In the 1851 census William Payne is listed as a 67-year-old farmer (which he probably had always been as well as being a landowner, copyholder and leasee). His wife Elizabeth (William Morris's mother) has died, aged 59, in May 1849 and is buried at Stoke St Gregory alongside her Hembrow/Morris relatives.

So in the 1851 census, Payne is listed as a widower and the farm he's on (though unnamed) is narrowed down to being in

---

4 - There is a fourth possibility – the records office in Exeter where it might have been kept was bombed during WWII and many records were lost

West Lyng. He has two female servants living with him and two male farm labourers. William and Ann's eldest son, William Payne Morris, now aged 13, is again listed as part of his household on that date. This may be a coincidence, but it is unlikely.

In the same census William Morris and Ann are also listed as farmers in West Lyng they are 34 and 38-years-old respectively and their two daughters, Elizabeth and Emma Ann are home, as are the two youngest boys Edwin Hy (age 2) and Edward S (born earlier that year). Jane Goodland and Charles Russell are listed as servants. Mary Bellamy aged 78 is visiting.

***

Sometime around 1854 William and Ann move to East Lydeard Farm, located on the outskirts of Bishops Lydeard village. The farm was part of the Sandhill Estate and at 280 acres it was quite large for the time so the rent would have been quite high. It's highly conceivable, based on details in Payne's will, that Payne and William Morris pooled assets and Payne moved with them to East Lydeard and retired from farming.

This is the last Will and Testament of me William Payne late of Lyng but now of Bishops Lydeard in the County of Somerset, Gentleman is follows. I give and bequeath unto William Morris the younger, Son of my Niece Ann Morris, All and every portion of my Household furniture, Plate, Linen, China, Glass, Books, and pictures that I may be possessed of at the Time of my decease for his own absolute use and benefit. I also give and bequeath unto the said William Morris the younger the Sum of Two Hundred Pounds of lawful British Money to be paid to him by my Trustees and Executors hereinafter named on his arriving to the age of Twenty one years and in the meantime Interest for the same as hereinafter mentioned — I give devise and bequeath unto William Morris the Elder of Bishops Lydeard and John Kidner of Thurlexton both in the said County of Somerset, Yeomen their Heirs, executors, administrators and assigns. All my Freehold, Leasehold, and Copyhold Messuages or Dwellinghouses, Lands, Tenements, and Hereditaments, whatsoever and wheresoever with their respective rights, members, and appurtenances And all my Monies and Securities for Money real and personal Estate whatsoever to which I or any person or persons in Trust for me, am are or is seized possessed or entitled or which I have power to give or dispose of by this my Will except what I have hereinbefore given and bequeathed to the said William Morris (the younger) And all other my Estate whatsoever and wheresoever in possession, reversion, remainder, or expectancy with the appurtenances to hold the said Freehold, Leasehold and Copyhold Messuages, Dwellinghouses, Lands, Tenements and Hereditaments Real and Personal Estate whatsoever and wheresoever as aforesaid Unto and to the use of the said William Morris, and John Kidner their Heirs, executors, administrators and assigns for ever according to the nature of the said Estates respectively Upon Trust nevertheless as hereinafter contained of and concerning the same, that is to say, Upon Trust that they the said William Morris and John Kidner or the Survivor of them or the Heirs executors administrators or assigns of such Survivor do and shall as soon after my decease as they can conveniently do so by one or more Sale or Sales absolutely sell and dispose of and convert into Money either together or in parcels and in such lot or Lots as they my said Trustees for the time being of this my Will may deem most eligible, and with liberty to buy in and resell the same at his or their discretion without being accountable for any diminution of price all and singular my said Freehold, Leasehold, and Copyhold, Messuages or Dwellinghouses, Lands, Tenements, Hereditaments and Premises with their

Page one of four and a half pages of William Payne's will – signed and dated 13 February 1856 – starts with the words…This is the last will and testament of one William Payne late of Lyng, but now of Bishops Lydeard. The will was witnessed by Isaac Palmer Smith and Anna Smith – who signed her name with an X.

He would be 70 years old when William and Ann move and he dies three years later, his death recorded as occurring in Bishops Lydeard.

In his will, William Payne bequeaths all his personal possessions to William and Ann's eldest son – William Payne Morris – confirming the relationship he had with both Williams. He was also bequeathed 'six hundred pounds of lawful pocket money' (the equivalent of just over 90,000 pounds in 2024) when he reached the age of 21, which he turns one year later in 1858.

It's a substantial bequest and had to be honoured before any other – I think it heavily implies that William Payne Morris had been adopted as Payne's heir. I have based this assumption on the fact Payne and Elizabeth had no children of their own to inherit their estate. William was listed as a member of Payne's household in the previous two census, he inherited all of Payne's belongings and has Payne as part of his name.

Payne did have a lot more to give however… William Morris (William P Morris's father) and John Kidner (from another big and long-standing farming family in West Somerset and probably the husband of one of Payne's sisters) were Payne's executors.

The sale of Payne's properties went ahead in February 1858 and information I found lists meadows, arable plots, pasture and orchards tenanted by various farmers – including the Jeanes (who came into our family), the Dare's, the Kidner's and CR Morris (a well-known auctioneer from a separate Morris family). Most of Payne's property was around North Curry but he had the following in Bishops Hull…

> *Messrs. Maynard and Sons, at the Old Inn, Bishops Hull, on Thursday, the 25th day of February instant, at the hour of five o'clock in the afternoon precisely, subject to conditions to be them produced, the undermentioned valuable dwelling-houses, gardens and premises, situated in the village of Bishops Hull, in the following, or such other lots as shall be named at the time of sale, viz: -*
>
> *1. All that well-frequented Dwelling-house and Inn, with the yard and premises behind the same, in the occupation of Mr John Macy, as tenant thereof.*

2. *All those two comfortable dwelling houses with the gardens and premises in front of the same, now in the occupation of Mr Clapp and Mr Gourd as tenants.*

3. *All that convenient brick built dwelling house, with two good walled gardens, and appurtenances thereto belonging, now in the occupation of Mr John Abbott, as tenant.*

The tenure of the above premises is customary freehold of inheritance, parcel of the Manor of Taunton Deane.... Further particulars may be obtained by Mr John Kidner, Thurloxton and Mr William Morris, East Lydeard[5].

---

5 - Taunton Courier and Western Advertiser – 17 February 1858

William Payne Morris son of William and Ann (Bellamy) Morris

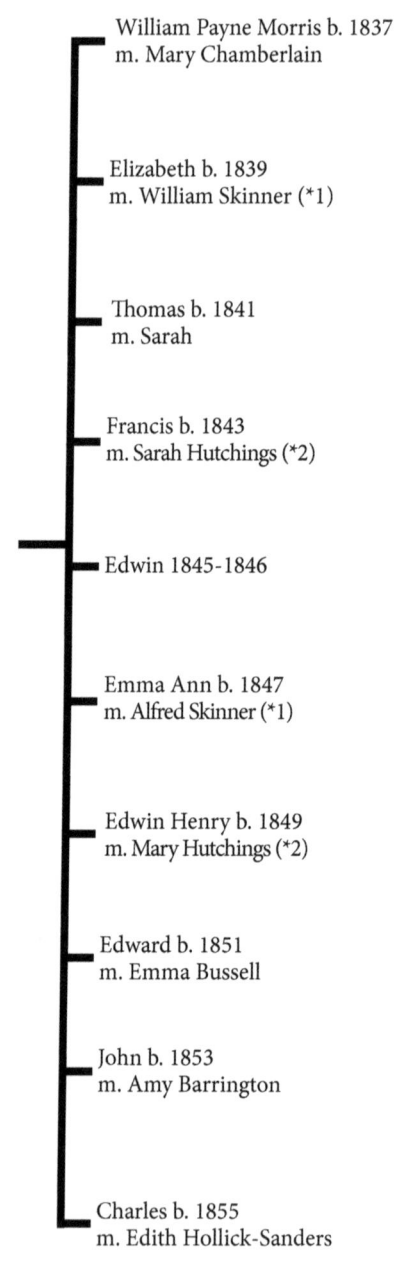

William Payne Morris b. 1837
m. Mary Chamberlain

Elizabeth b. 1839
m. William Skinner (*1)

Thomas b. 1841
m. Sarah

Francis b. 1843
m. Sarah Hutchings (*2)

Edwin 1845-1846

Emma Ann b. 1847
m. Alfred Skinner (*1)

Edwin Henry b. 1849
m. Mary Hutchings (*2)

Edward b. 1851
m. Emma Bussell

John b. 1853
m. Amy Barrington

Charles b. 1855
m. Edith Hollick-Sanders

* siblings

William and Ann (formerly Bellamy) Morris – the East Lydeard Farm years
c1854 – 1883

It seems likely William and Ann moved to East Lydeard Farm sometime around early 1854 if I use the baptism records of their children as a guide. Their ninth child and second youngest son, John, had been baptised, in the same Lyng church as the other children, in 1853. Then the youngest son, Charles, is recorded as being born in East Lydeard in 1855.

A newspaper article from June 1854 reports on a petty sessions case in which a Charles Yeandle was accused of stealing two bushels of wheat (value — 18 shillings) the property of William Morris, at Bishops Lydeard, on the 7th day of April, 1854. Charles Yeandle was acquitted but the information in the article places the family at East Lydeard Farm in 1854[6].

By 1843 Taunton was connected to the national railway system as part of the Bristol and Exeter railway designed by Isambard Kingdom Brunel. The arrival of the railways made an enormous difference to the way people and products moved around the countryside. The number of journeys made by train in 1843 was 23 million; seven years later, in 1850, it had more than tripled to 73 million. For farmers, and indeed all industry, it was becoming easier to move and sell produce. Changes in agriculture too had been dramatic over the past century – sheep were nearly three times the weight and cattle twice what they had been 100 years before.

Even to be a tenant you had to have a lot of upfront capital. East Lydeard Farm when it sold in 1913 was being rented for £488, 15s. 6d. per annum (this is nearly 40,000 pounds in 2024), there is no reason to believe it would have been any cheaper in 1854. It was rented to the same person for at least a year. The cost included the lease, apportioned rent and

---

6 - Taunton Courier and Western Advertiser – Wednesday 28 June 1854

tithes (a payment from medieval times to the Church) and a sporting rent (to enable you to hunt rabbits and deer etc).

Once rent was paid you could farm as you wished in order to pay the rent for the following year and hopefully make a living. Due to the size of East Lydeard Farm you also became an employer.

According to the census of 1861, where the family name is misspelled as Moris (accuracy is still not strong) there was a household of eleven people living at East Lydeard Farm. William is 48-years-old and Ann would be around 50. Most of the older children – William Payne, Elizabeth, Francis, Emma and Edward – are home, but Thomas, Edwin, John and Charles are not. A Frederick Moris (sp) is also there aged 0 and listed as a son – I think it's more likely he's a cousin given Ann's age and because his name is not recorded in the family bible. Frances Hallock and Henry Young of Bishops Lydeard live at the farm as a milkmaid and carter along with Simon Slade also a carter. It's a big and expensive household.

Despite the country side being an easier place to live than the cities in the 1850s and 60s, times were tough for ordinary people.

Given the struggle to make ends meet it's not surprising that in the course of the next few years we see William, either giving evidence or laying accusations at the Petty Sessions Court in Bishops Lydeard. In 1858 Thomas Pugsley was caught and convicted of stealing two pecks of peas from East Lydeard and sentenced to 14 days hard labour at Taunton jail.

At the Petty Sessions in February 1867 15-year-old Mary Ann Burston is charged by William Morris over the stealing of a pint of milk. She apparently brought her brother's breakfast to the farm every day and on this day was caught stealing a pint of milk from the dairy…it seems a small offence and she was not punished but *'discharged on her father becoming surety for her good behaviour for three months.'*[7]

Which may not have been such a good idea because Samuel Burston (aged 50 and therefore likely to be her father) and his son 24-year-old James Burston were caught by the local policeman, Sergeant Everleigh having stolen four fowls. *After hearing the evidence of Mr Morris, Mrs Morris and Sergt. Everleigh, both prisoners were committed for trial.*[8]

---

7 - West Somerset Free Press – Saturday 16 February 1867
8 - Western Gazette – Friday 10 January 1868

1867 was also the year that a law was passed making it illegal for children under 8-years-of-age to be employed by agricultural gangs. They had, up until then, hired children out to pick fruit, weed fields, thin turnips etc, working them long hours and paying only pennies.

Poaching was also an issue and still a crime with serious consequences no matter the hardship. In February 1868…

> *'Richard Board, jun., Thomas Sandins and Uriah Culverwell, were charged by William Eveleigh, under gamekeeper to Lord Kensington, with trespassing in pursuit of game on land in the occupation of Mr. William. Morris, East Lydeard Farm, the 29th of January. — William Eveleigh stated that on the day in question he was crossing a field in the occupation of Mr. Morris, called Eighteen Acres, when saw the defendant with two dogs, trying a hedge. As soon as they saw the witness they went towards a pond, where they saw Board take something from under his slop and hide it amongst the bushes. The witness afterwards went to the pond and found a small black bag, containing hare and a rabbit, quite warm. He called to the defendants, and Board*

and Culverwell went back. He asked them how they got the hare and rabbit, and Board said, "The old bitch caught the hare up in the hollow ground, and that, is where the rabbit was caught." Board and Culverwell were each fined with 8s. costs, or two months' hard labour. Sandins was fined £1 and 8s. costs, or one month's hard labour.' [9]

These examples help to demonstrate life was hard for everyone, especially the poor, but it was the children who mostly suffered the consequences. Until the early 1900s, for every 1000 children 154 did not live to adulthood. William and Ann sadly did not escape the national average. Of their 10 children a son, Edwin, died in infancy in 1846. School was not compulsory until the 1880s when children from the ages of 5 to 10 years were expected to attend classes (which ironically killed more of them because of the spread of disease in the over-crowded classrooms) William and Ann, however, valued education and all their children including the girls Elizabeth and Emma Ann – at least for a while – attended classes. Both daughters are listed as scholars, meaning they

---

9 - West Somerset Free Press – Saturday 22 February 1868

were at school or at least having lessons, in the 1851 census. Many of the boys were sent away to school, sometimes small local ones but also Queens in Taunton and the Devon County School.

Elizabeth Morris Skinner eldest daughter
of William and Ann (Bellamy) Morris

- William Payne Morris b. 1837
  m. Mary Chamberlain

- Elizabeth b. 1839
  m. William Skinner (*1)

- Thomas b. 1841
  m. Sarah

- Francis b. 1843
  m. Sarah Hutchings (*2)

- Edwin 1845-1846

- Emma Ann b. 1847
  m. Alfred Skinner (*1)

- Edwin Henry b. 1849
  m. Mary Hutchings (*2)

- Edward b. 1851
  m. Emma Bussell

- John b. 1853
  m. Amy Barrington

- Charles b. 1855
  m. Edith Hollick-Sanders

The Children Of William and Ann

Details of the ten children of William and Ann Morris are as follows:

William Payne Morris: Was born on 24 September, 1837 and baptised in Lyng. On 2 July, 1862 he marries 19-year-old Mary Burton Chamberlain at Whimple in Devon. She is the eldest daughter of John Chamberlain of Lower Stenton House in Whimple. They move to Combe Down Farm in Combe Florey and have multiple children. He has an interesting trajectory – being declared bankrupt at one point despite his large inheritance from William Payne and his children have interesting lives in Somerset and elsewhere. He dies in 1909 possibly in Bishops Hull.

Elizabeth Morris: Was born 2 June 1839 and baptised in Lyng. On 3 December, 1862 she marries William Comer Skinner at the church in Bishops Lydeard. He is also from a very long-standing Somerset farming family. They live at Howleigh Farm in Pitminster and also have many children – they take over the tenancy of East Lydeard Farm for 20 years (from 1884 – 1904) after William Morris dies. Elizabeth dies in 1908 at the age of 69 and is buried in Bishops Lydeard as is her husband William Skinner who lived to the ripe old age of 92, dying in 1925.

Thomas Morris: Was born on 31 March, 1841. Sometime in the middle of the 1860s having done an apprenticeship in Exeter as a butcher, he goes to Australia where he marries and has four children. We know this because his youngest brother, Charles, left Thomas's two sons and two daughters 500 pounds each in his will in 1926.

There's a listing for a Thomas Morris setting sail for Melbourne in 1864 from Plymouth on a ship called the Clyde arriving in Australia on 21 June, 1864. Records in Melbourne show there was a Thomas Morris who was a butcher in Flemington (on the corner of Princes Street and Racecourse Road) who died in 1883 – making him 43. He had married – his wife Sarah was his sole beneficiary in his will. It makes no mention of children but, if he had any, they are likely to be under the age of 18 at this time. Charles Morris doesn't name Thomas's children in his will so I can't cross-reference.

Francis (Frank) Morris: Was born on 11 June 1843 and baptised in Lyng. He marries Sarah Ann Hutchings a farmer's daughter from Pitminster on 12 August, 1874. They start their farming life at Burge – a farm the other side of the railway line (opened in 1862) which ran from Taunton to Watchet, passing through Bishops Lydeard. Francis and Sarah moved in the 1880s to Norton Court Farm close to Conquest and Portman. They had five children. Their three daughters never marry and live together most of their lives in Milverton, the eldest, Elinor, was alive and living in Taunton until 1966. Francis dies aged 80 at Dipford Farm in Trull in 1930.

Emma Ann Morris: Was born 4 April, 1847 in Lyng. On 9 October, 1872 she marries Alfred Skinner, the brother of William Comer Skinner who had married her sister

Elizabeth. He farms at Pound, next door to East Lydeard, and is one of the country's top breeders of Devon cattle. Their story and that of their descendants could fill a book. Skinners remain at Pound Farm until 1950 when Emma Ann's youngest son, Gordon, sells it to Alan Herbert Morris, his cousin.

Edwin Henry Morris: Was born 10 May, 1849 in Lyng. On 23 November, 1876 he marries Mary Hutchings at Corfe Church. Mary was the younger sister of Sarah Ann Hutchings who had married Francis. In 1881 they are farming in Portman but then move to Kilton-cum-Lilstock for many years and end up at Doniford Farm near Watchet. They have one daughter Beatrice and adopt another girl, Evelyn Palmer, born in London when she's a baby (there's another story here). Edwin dies on 21 April, 1924.

Edward Morris: Was born 18 February, 1851 in Lyng. On 26 December, 1877, he marries Emma Bussell, daughter of a Taunton tailor at St Mary's church in Taunton. Edward had done an apprenticeship at a grocer's in Taunton and when he marries at 27 is listed as a tea merchant. Tea had arrived in England nearly two hundred years before but for many of those years had been too expensive for most ordinary people to drink. By the 1870s it was being grown throughout the colonies of India, Sri Lanka and East Africa and much more accessible and was probably very 'in fashion' at the time he married. Edward and Emma move to London – Finsbury Park – have many children and Edward dies aged 86 in 1937 in Stoke Newington.

John (Jack) Morris: (our Great-Grandfather): Was born on 2 March, 1853 and is the last child to be born in Lyng.

Charles Morris: Was born at East Lydeard on 1 March, 1855.

More details about John and Charles are included in the following pages.

This picture of East Lydeard Farm is taken in the early 1870's and probably shows William and Ann Bellamy/Morris with their two youngest sons, John and Charles Morris.

The 1870s Onwards

In September 1871 William and Ann's youngest son, Charles, finishes school at the Devon County School in West Buckland and starts an apprenticeship as an engineer with Edward Hayes at Stony Stratford in Buckinghamshire. Despite that company's distance from the sea, it was well-known for building steamboats and tugs that were used to explore everywhere from the jungles of South America to the Arctic, receiving commissions from people as diverse as the Shah of Iran, the Sultan of Morocco and the governments of Russia and Japan.

Then comes an annus horribilis (1873) for the family, all of whom become embroiled in a court case that is reported in great detail. It starts after Harriet Branchflower aged

15-years-old and living at East Lydeard Farm with her family – her father William works on the farm and her sister Mary works in the house. For several weeks in March 1872 Mary was too sick to work so her sister Harriet replaced her. Nine months later, in January 1873, Harriet gives birth to a son and claims Charles Morris is the father. She alleges that Charles raped her twice over the course of a week in March and threw her a shilling to keep quiet.

However, Charles lived in Stony Stratford in Buckinghamshire, from September 1871, doing his engineering apprenticeship. While he came home for Christmas absolutely no one (and everyone from his brothers, parents, employers and her family testified) witnessed him at East Lydeard Farm at all during that March. In fact, they all testified that he wasn't and couldn't have been there.

Two other brothers were at the farm. John was living at the farm and working with his father and Edward was an apprentice living and working in Taunton at a grocers but came home some weekends. When all the brothers stood in a line together in the court room it was noted how alike they looked. But Harriet continued to insist the father of her son was Charles…which, given everyone's testimony, it couldn't have been.

When Charles was acquitted, it must have been a huge relief to the family but for the Branchflowers it was disastrous. Harriet's father, William, was really the only member of the family who stood with her and as a result he was sent to jail. Harriet also went to jail for several weeks. It is most likely that the rest of Harriet's family, with limited means to support themselves, were consigned to the Workhouse. How, why and what really happened is not clear and some Branchflowers were employed by other members of the family even after the case concluded.

***

In 1878 Charles leaves his employer, Edward Hayes, having long finished his apprenticeship and works briefly for J and H Mclaren in Hunslet Leeds. He then moves to John Fowlers and Company and is posted by them to Calcutta (Kolkata) in India.

Meanwhile back in Bishops Lydeard, according to the 1881 census, William is still farming East Lydeard – and he's employing four men and five boys. Their only child still at home is our great-grandfather, John who's 28. Herbert Skinner – Emma Ann and Alfred's son aged 5 is also staying with them.

The End of an Era

William dies on 23 January, 1883 at East Lydeard. He is 65 years old. He leaves a beautifully written and interesting will.

His first direction was to have everything he owned (furniture/crops/machinery) and the two farms he tenanted – East Lydeard and Portman, owned by Sir Wroth Lethbridge – valued by local auctioneer Mr Cuthbert Morris (no relation)…

> *And subject to my said wife having the use of such of my furniture to the value of 40 pounds as she may select during her life, and subject to my said son John maintaining my said wife and providing her with a comfortable home and all necessaries*

during her life, or if she shall prefer to live separate from my said son then subject to his paying her the sum of thirty shillings a week to be paid weekly or once every four weeks as my son may think fit during her life and also subject to my said son paying all necessary expenses attending my wife's funeral, I give and bequeath my said live and dead farming stock, crops, furniture, chattels and effects and also the advantage and benefit of my tenancies in the farms which I shall be renting at the time of my decease unto my said son. But I declare that if the valuation of my said farming stock, crops, furniture, tenancies and effects shall exceed the sum of nine hundred pounds after deducting all debts, rents and other liabilities due from me at the date of my decease and also my funeral and testamentary expenses then my said son shall pay to my son-in-law, William Comer Skinner, within a period of two years from the date of my decease but without interest the amount of the valuation in excess of the said sum of nine hundred pounds[10]....

---

10 - Last Will and Testament of William Morris (1871-1883)

> This is the last Will and Testament of me William Morris of East Lydeard in the County of Somerset Yeoman I appoint my wife Ann Morris and my son John Morris joint Executors of this my Will. I direct my said executors immediately on my death to have my live and dead farming stock crops and other farming effects and household furniture on East Lydeard and Broman farms now rented by me of his Wroth Lethbridge or upon any other farms which may be rented by me at the time of my decease and all other my chattels (including the advantage and benefit of my Tenancies if such Terms) valued by Mr Cuthbert Haddam Morris of North Curry in the said County of Somerset if he be living at the time of my decease or if not then by some other competent person And subject to my said wife having the use of such of my furniture to the value of forty pounds as she may select during her life And subject to my said son maintaining my said wife and providing her with a comfortable home and all necessaries during her life or if she shall prefer to live separate from my said son then subject to his paying her the sum of thirty shillings a week to be paid weekly or once every four weeks as my son may think fit during her life And also subject to my said son paying all necessary expenses attending my wife's funeral I give and bequeath my said live and dead farming stock crops furniture chattels and effects and also the advantage and benefit of my Tenancies in the farms which I shall be renting at the time of my decease unto my said son But I declare that if the valuation of my said farming stock crops furniture tenancies and effects shall exceed the sum of nine hundred pounds after deducting all debts rents and other liabilities due from me at the date of my decease and also my funeral and testamentary expenses then my said son shall pay to my son in law William Corner Skinner within a period of two years from the date of my decease but without interest the amount of the valuation in excess of the said sum of nine hundred pounds but if my said son John shall give up my said farms or either of them within the said period of two years from my decease then such excess shall become due and payable to my said son in law on the determination of the Tenancy of the said farms or of such of the said farms as shall be so given up by my said son And I give and bequeath such excess subject and in manner aforesaid unto the said William Corner Skinner accordingly All the residue of

William's wife, Ann Bellamy/Morris, and his son, our great-grandfather, John Morris were the executors.

At the time of William's death nine of his children were still alive yet his will only makes provision for his wife, Ann, son John (who was farming with him) and son-in-law, William Comer Skinner (Elizabeth's husband)…why? What follows is a period of family members moving around.

Four months after William's death, on 19 April, 1883, most of the stock, crops and some farm implements from East Lydeard Farm are sold at auction and John and his mother move to Portman Farm. William Comer Skinner and his wife Elizabeth move to East Lydeard Farm and take on the tenancy for the next two decades until April 1904 when William Skinner retires.

On 4 November, 1888 Charles marries Edith Hollick Sanders at St Giles Church, Stony Stratford. His address is listed as Russel Street, Calcutta on the wedding certificate.

Also in 1888 there's an auction at Conquest Farm and it's most likely that this is when John Morris (our great-grandfather) also took on that tenancy. In the census of 1891 John is single, aged 37-years-old, and is head of the household while living as a farmer at Portman. His mother Ann is 77 and listed as 'living on her own means' also at Portman.

Ann Morris dies on 24 December, 1892 at Portman Cottage. Seven years later, in June 1899, John moves to Conquest after a fire destroys the Portman farmhouse along with many other buildings.

DESTRUCTIVE FIRE AT BISHOP'S LYDEARD. FARM – HOUSE BURNT DOWN •£1,500 DAMAGE

A fire of a very destructive character occurred Portman Farm, Bishop's Lydeard, on Tuesday afternoon, and resulted in the total destruction of the fine old farm-house, besides the partial demolition of a mill, a barn, and various outbuildings. The house was occupied Mr. John Morris, a farmer well known in West Somerset, and the owner of the property is Sir Wroth Acland Lethbridge, of Sandhill Park. Bishops Lydeard.

Mr. Morris was engaged with his men on Tuesday about noon in sacking corn in a barn about thirty feet from the dwelling-house. The corn had to be delivered at Watchet the same day, but this will never be possible, as it is now reduced to heaps of black dust. While Mr. Morris was engaged in this operation one of his domestic servants rushed to him and told him that the furnace chimney, which is situated at the end of the house, had caught fire. Mr. Morris and his men proceeded the spot and found, to their dismay, that the sparks from the chimney had ignited the thatch roof, and it was not long before there was a great blaze.

There were only five men working in the vicinity of the house at the time, and these did their utmost to arrest the progress of the fire, but owing to their small number their efforts were not of much avail.

A telegram was therefore dispatched to the captain of the Taunton Fire Brigade to come immediately, and meanwhile the men directed their energies to saving the large quantity of valuable furniture which was in the house. In this they were extremely successful, for the whole or it, or almost the whole of it, was got out, and placed upon the lawn and the adjoining ground.

The telegram reached Captain Coles five minutes past one, and says much for the energy and celerity of the brigade that they were playing upon the flames at Bishops Lydeard just twenty minutes later. When the brigade arrived they found the dwelling-house, which is about fifty feet long, burning from end to end, but the roof was not yet in. The fall of this, however, soon occurred, though as it was thatch all efforts to save it were necessarily futile. The burning house presented a woeful sight, and the extent and power of the flames may be judged from the fact that they leapt across an intervening space of thirty feet and caught the barn, and then spread to the adjoining cowsheds.

It was hot day, but the fire-brigade men worked with a will, and were very efficiently aided by about fifty willing helpers, including labourers from the adjoining farms. Mr A. C. Skinner, of Pound. Mr. W. H. Burston, of Fitzroy farm, and Mr. Walter Lickfold, of Bishop's Lydeard. were also to the fore with wise advice and help. There was, fortunately, a splendid supply of water, which was obtained from the mill-tail, and this was kept pouring with might and main through the four lengths of hose. The men worked incessantly for five hours, and Capt. Coles and his firemen were highly praised for the valuable result they were able to accomplish. The farm-house became a total wreck, as also did the barn where Mr. Morris and his employees had been engaged in sacking corn. A second barn, a loft, a cottage, the whole of the cowsheds, part of the mill-house, wagon-house, about 25 tons of hay, and another rick were fortunately saved. The damage amounts to about 1,500 pounds, and the property is insured in the Atlas Fire Office. The value the property which was saved cannot be less than 600 or 700 pounds. There is one curious incident worthy of mention. While engaged in sacking the corn. Mr, Morris took off his waistcoat, as the day was hot, and put it on one side. In one of the pockets of this was his valuable gold watch, which was an heirloom from his father; and upon which he naturally set great store. This was quite forgotten in the excitement which ensued, and the barn, in which the waistcoat had been set down in, was burnt down. In searching among the debris in the evening, however, the watch was found, and, wonderful to relate, it was uninjured, and was still going, while the chain was utterly destroyed. The watch must, apparently, have got embedded, in falling material, and have been marvellously protected by this. The corn in the barn was converted into a charred mass.

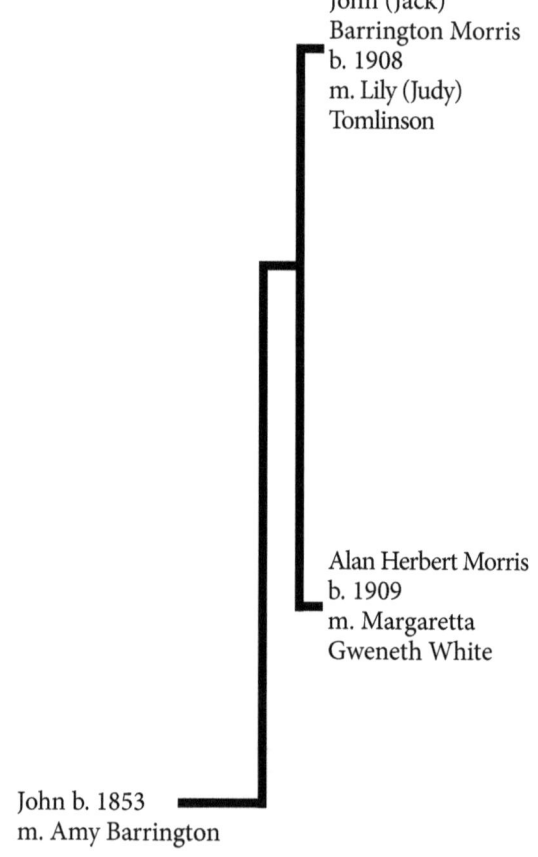

Into the 1900s

By the 1901 census John is still single at 47-years-of-age and living back at Portman. He has a housekeeper, Bessie Palfrey. Bessie Holland is a servant, Richard Willcocks is the stockman and James Mogridge aged 14 is the 'boy working on the farm'.

During the previous decade Charles Morris remained in Calcutta, rising to the position of Chairman at Jessops – an Indian engineering firm – and as a result had become very wealthy. In September 1901 Charles buys Highfield Hall, a huge estate in Hertfordshire.

> *Messrs. Gibson have disposed of the Highfield Hall estate (Sept 1901), near St Albans, to Mr C Morris, a Calcutta merchant, who has recently returned*

to England and intends to settle in this neighbourhood. The estate was purchased by a London syndicate from Mrs East with the intention of developing it for the erection of high-class villas. Mr Morris, however, has bought the whole estate, and we are informed the he will demolish the present house and build one of a more palatial type in its place. [11]

***

Six years after Charles buys Highfield Hall a Mr E B Tavender discovered Alfred Skinner (husband of Emma Ann) lying where he had fallen from his horse. Mr Tavender was the tenant of East Lydeard Farm from 1904 until 1913. Alfred died a few days after his fall and his funeral in Bishops Lydeard was attended by around 500 people from all walks of life. As his coffin made its way down Pound Lane on a funeral horse and cart, the lane and the main street to the church were lined with people.

DEATH OF MR. A. C. SKINNER (Sept 1906). The death took place on Monday evening at his residence, Pound Farm,

---

11 - West Somerset Free Press – Saturday 3 June 1899

Bishop's Lydeard, near Taunton, of Mr. Alfred C. Skinner, j.p., c.c, who was well-known throughout the West of England as a noted breeder of Devon cattle, and successful exhibitor at the leading shows throughout the country. Mr. Skinner was returning home last Thursday night from visit he had paid to Mr. Samuel Kidner, at Milverton, and when near his residence his horse shied at, it is supposed, some running water in the roadway. Mr. Skinner was discovered about midnight lying on the road by Mr. E B Tavender, another farmer of East Lydeard, who was cycling home after seeing Taunton Carnival.[12]

Alfred Skinner is someone who was large in the community, not just well-known for being one of the top breeders of Devon Cattle, but also for his work with the church and in the community of Bishops Lydeard.

The Pound Herd of Devon Cattle (July 1891). *The neighbourhood of Bishop's Lydeard has from the earliest records been the home of noted breeders of Devon cattle. Lying on the borders of the rich Vale of Taunton, and almost under the shadow of the Quantock Hills, the soil and climate conducive to their healthy*

---

12 - Luton Times and Advertiser – Friday 20 September 1901

growth and robust development, whilst the herds thereabout can claim strong infusion of the best blood which has ever been registered, and race to the oldest stocks of which there are any records. One of the largest and most important of these is that at Pound farm. which has been bred by Mr Alfred C Skinner since 1859. This herd, however, has been in the family for many years, Mr John Skinner having brought it to Pound farm in 1844 from Pitpear in the parish of Ash Priors, he being the sixth John Skinner in succession who had owned that estate. It is believed that all these gentlemen were breeders of Devon cattle, but, at all event, it was a generation old when removed to its present home in 1844, and since the death of John Skinner in 1859 his son, Mr A C Skinner who took the management of the farm in 1862, and became sole owner of the entire herd in 1872 and has brought it into great prominence. Devon breeders of to-day are all familiar with the marked successes achieved by him in the best show yards of the country since he first began exhibiting, in 1877. [13]

---

13 - Taunton Courier and Advertiser – Wednesday 15 July 1891

Charles Morris used Alfred's cattle as the basis for his pedigree herd of Devon Cattle that were starting to be exported around the world from Highfield and later East Lydeard at around this time.

Alfred's widow, Emma Ann Skinner took up the herd with her son Gordon, who was 21 at the time of his father's death. As one of the only women exhibitors of cattle in her own right – her name – Mrs A C Skinner and son – is listed among the prize winners at many county shows. It should also be noted that she bought Pound Farm.

On 24 July, 1907 at the age of 53, our Great-Grandfather John marries Amy Barrington at Creech St Michael – she is 26 and a farmer's daughter from the village of Ham with five sisters and a brother. They have two children:

John Barrington Morris (our grandfather) was born at Conquest on 28 April, 1908.

Alan Herbert Morris (our great-uncle) was born on 14 May, 1909 also at Conquest.

This is possibly a wedding picture for John and Amy Barrington/Morris – Charles Morris is on the far right – but all the male faces have enough similarities to be able to say they are family (I think).

1913 – A Year Of Great Change

This is the year that the Morris family move from being tenant farmers to farm owners and the Sandhill Estate (the largest in West Somerset) is broken up and put up for sale… All the farms bought in the sale except Conquest are still in the Morris family (as of 2024).

SOMERSET ESTATE. SANDHILL SALE. (Oct 1913).

The sale of the Sandhill Park Estate, near Taunton, the property of Sir Wroth Lethbridge, Bart., has been held at Taunton. The lots, numbering 134, comprised Sandhill Park House. The auctioneers were Messrs. Millar, Son, and Co., of Pall Mall, London, while the solicitors engaged were Messrs.

Hoaseman and Co., of Parliament Chambers, Westminster, London. The auctioneers acted in conjunction with Messrs. Morris, Sons, and Peard, of North Curry, Taunton. Mr. William G. Millar conducted the sale. The following were among- the lots disposed of the day before yesterday-. —The Longlands Farm, close to Bishop's Lydeard Station, 85 acres, rental 183pds let to Mr. Thomas Triggol, sold to the tenant at £3,725. **Conquest Farm, on the main Taunton road to Bishop's Lydeard, 127 acres, rental £257, let to Mr. John Morris, sold to the tenant at £5,250.** *Tatham Farm, Bishop's Lydeard, described by the auctioneer as more like a garden than a farm, 102 acres, rental £272, let to Mr. J. T. Hearn, purchased by Mr. H Wills, of Wrington, for £6,000.* **East Lydeard Farm, Bishop's Lydeard, 281 acres, £488, let to Mr. E. B. Tavender, sold at £9,500 to Messrs. Sweet and Son, solicitors, Taunton, on behalf of a client, Pound Farm, Bishop's Lydeard, for many years occupied by the late Mr. A. C. Skinner the noted Devon cattle breeder, 260 acres, rental £495, let to Mrs. A. C. Skinner, sold to the tenant at £11,000.** [14]

---

14 - Exeter and Plymouth Gazette – Tuesday 2 October 1913

Sandhill Park Estate. Important property sale at Taunton – tenant farmers become owners: (Oct 1913)…
Lot 2 – Conquest Farm, abutting on the main Taunton Road, with stone-built residence and substantial farm buildings, and two newly erected brick and tiled cottages. The land lies in a ring fence and is well watered, and dividing into highly fertile and valuable enclosures of meadow, pasture, orchard and arable, extending to an area of about 127a. 2r. 15p. Let to Mr John Morris at the annual rent of 257 pds 17s 9d per annum. Bidding commenced at 4,000 and rose by 250 bids to 5,000, the tenant, Mr John Morris being the purchaser at 5,250pds.

Lot 3 – Portman Farm, *adjoining Conquest Farm, with stone and tiled farmhouse, recently erected as two cottages, but planned for conversion. The farm buildings are substantial and suitable for the holding. Another cottage of four rooms, and a good water supply. The land exends to an area of about 128a 2r 13p. Let to Mr John Morris at the annual apportioned rent of 236pds 0s 2d per annum. This lot was put up in the sum of 2,500 and was withdrawn at 4,000....It was, in subsequent days, bought by John Morris as well.* [15]

---

15 - Taunton Courier and Western Advertiser – 22 October 1913

East Lydeard Farm was sold to solicitors in Taunton on behalf of a client, who was Charles Morris. This was the place he had been born and he wanted a connection to the area and his family. It was also conveniently far away from Highfield so he could split his herd of Devon cattle, hoping it would mean if one herd came down with foot and mouth (which was rife at this time) the other would stay unaffected.

It's hard to figure out exactly how many members of the extended family fought in the First World War but three certainly did. William Inman Morris (grandson of William Payne Morris) signed up in 1914 and died of a gunshot wound to the pelvis compounded by pneumonia in a military hospital at Mount Vernon on 11 February, 1916. He is buried in Hampstead Cemetery with other family members. Another grandson of William P Morris, Sydney Peters, signed up early to the 1st West Somerset Yeomanry. He died in August 1915 at his home, Parsonage Farm, Bishops Hull. He came home on leave to help plant spring crops, and was too sick after he returned to his unit to go to Gallipoli with them so was sent home again and tragically died of septicaemia. He was buried with full military honours at St

Mary's Church in Taunton aged 23. Edward 'Howard' Skinner – youngest son of Emma Ann Morris/Skinner and Alfred C Skinner – died in the first battle of the Somme on 20 September 1916. He is buried at the Guard's Cemetery in Lesboeufs.

Highfield Hall became in part a nursing home and after 30 years of marriage Edith Hollick Sanders/Morris dies at Highfield in June 1915 at age 58. She and Charles had no children.

In 1920 Charles donated two recreation fields – one in the nearby village of Tyttenhanger and, a larger one, off White Horse Lane for London Colney. In 1922 he gave another plot of land in Tyttenhanger for a 'social club', which still exists and can still be rented.

By the early 1920s Charles was world-renowned for his Devon cattle.

MR CHARLES MORRIS'S FARM AND DEVON CATTLE. (June 1923)

There is one name of outstanding fame in the Devon world to-day, and that is Mr Charles Morris, Highfield Hall, St. Alban's. Now, this keen, shrewd breeder of Devons has the merit of not always having remained at home. He first saw the light at East Lydeard Farm, Bishop's Lydeard and when he now comes down to Somerset he sleeps in the same bedroom in which he was born. He tells the tale of how, when he was a youth, he took the team of horses and wagon to Watchet, loaded it up with, sea washed kidney cobbles, and then cemented them to make a real West Country walk to the front door. Ah," he says, I would have made that path smoother as a youth if I had known what it meant to walk on it with increase of age."

Then Mr Morris went to India, and his fine Somerset built constitution stuck the climate well. When he settled down at St. Albans, he had still a hankering for the cattle of his youth and he founded the 'Highfield' herd by making selections from the finest herds of the West. He skilfully got his specimen Devons, and blended them into the now highly redoubtable herd, whose prize-winning record is increased by each show visited.

Being a business man, he saw that it was no use to accumulate stocks without an outlet, and he started to develop an export trade, and has sent out upwards of 100 Devons per annum to Australia, New

Zealand, India, the Argentine, Uruguay, Patagonia, Venezuela, Guatemala, and other parts of South America, South Africa, Rhodesia, and Europe.

If he gets on the track of a good Devon he is as purposeful in securing it as a weazel (sic) after rabbit. I have given a brief resume of Mr Morris and his Highfield connections, but because of the occasional outbreaks of foot-and-mouth disease in England militated his filling, by reason of the regulations, all the shipping orders he received, he determined to add to his responsibilities by securing the old home at East Lydeard for the purpose of founding a second herd there.

This farm comprises 283 acres and is the acme of good management. Practically half of it is arable, and on these acres are grown wheat and beans. Then there were the fodder crops with the trifolium just showing its crimson head, and the rest of the farm is grass. Mr Morris was fortunate in securing the services Mr J. R. Glanfield as manager, and he has everything at his fingertips.

Now it is here the idea that though milk must not be lost sight of, the item to be secured is a large frame clothed with a wealth of flesh. Here lies the secret of Mr Morris's success and the open-air pasturage. Before referring to the cattle, I might mention that I had one of these somewhat should-like-to possess'em feelings as I looked at his fine flock of Dorset Horn sheep. About 140 ewes are lambed early. His pen of three just walked over at Bath, and was first also at the Bath and West at Swansea. He also keeps some Large Black pigs at grass.

Then I had a glance at his show cattle. How healthy they were kept! Even the sheds were open to the air at the back. There was that beautiful three-year-old Lottie 3rd. She has scored right through. Then there was the superb cow Highfield Farthing 8th. What a record for the only times shown—1st, Devon County Exeter, 1920; lst. Royal Cornwall. Callington; 1st Royal Agricultural Society, Darlington. In 1921 she went on with first and champion Devon County. Tavistock; Ist and champion, Bath and West, Bristol; lst and champion, Royal Show at Derby; Ist and reserve champion. Bath and West Plymouth. 1922; lst prize. Somerset County Show, Bath. 1923; lst and reserve champion Bath and West, Swansea;

and she was also well in it at the Devon County Show at Bideford this week.

Mr C. Morris's exhibits also secured the Christie 30 guineas challenge cup for group of Devon cattle, one male and three females; also the President's challenge bowl for group of three female Devons, and the silver cup for cow or heifer. I could follow on enumerating Mr Morris's successes with his noted herd, but, like, all good men, he has an eye and a kindly thought for his fellows. The steer is the commercial sheet anchor of the breed and at a meeting of the Devon Cattle Breeders' Society in the show yard at Bideford on Tuesday, he carried a motion for an annual sale to be held under the auspices of the society, the first of which will be held at Exeter in April next. Such is Mr Charles Morris, his herd, and his farms, the man who has done so much to re-establish the Devon breed from outside favour, and bring with it the choicest sirloin in the world into its own again. ELDRED G. F. WALKER ("North Somerset")[16].

---

16 - Western Daily Press – Saturday 2 June 1923

Charles and our great grandfather, John known by the family as Jack, were close so it's fitting that one of the very few photographs we have of him are of the two brothers together.

John (Jack) Morris died 30 March, 1924 aged 71 at Conquest.

Bishops Lydeard (April 1924): *Death and Funeral of Mr John Morris. Keen sportsman and agriculturalist. Quite a surprise was caused on Sunday afternoon, when the tolling of the death bell brought the sad and unexpected news of the death of Mr John Morris of Conquest Farm, to the majority of the inhabitants. Mr Morris who was a native of the parish, was born at East Lydeard and lived there for some years, then moved to Portman with his mother, which was later burnt down. He then moved to Conquest where he married, and resided up to the time of his death, which occurred about two o'clock on Sunday from heart trouble. Although not being in the best of health for some time past, he was not seriously ill until within a week of his death, which was somewhat unexpected. He leaves a widow and two sons to mourn their loss and for whom the greatest sympathy is felt.*

The late Mr Morris was one of the keenest and best sportsmen in the district, and as a puppy walker it can safely be said that he had no equal. And by his death the

Taunton Vale Harriers and the Taunton Vale Foxhounds have lost a valued member. In 1913, on the sale of Sandhill Park Estate, he purchased both Portman and Conquest Farm which comprised about 400 acres, and upon which he had spent practically the whole of his life. He married some 17 or 18 years ago, Miss Barrington of Creech St Michael.

The Funeral *Took place at Bishops Lydeard on Thursday amid every sign of grief at the loss of a real friend, whom many described as one of the real "old sort". As the cortege slowly proceeded from Conquest Farm to the churchyard, many gave token of the grief they felt, whilst a large congregation had assembled to do honour to the memory of a true friend.*

The body was enclosed in an unpolished oak coffin, with heavy brass fittings, and the engraved plate bore the inscription:- "John Morris, died March 30th, 1924, aged 71 years." [17]

Our grandfather John/Jack was nearly 15 at the time. It seems he probably continued at

---

17 - Taunton Courier and Western Advertiser – Wednesday 9 April 1924

school. His brother Alan wrote diaries all his life and a few are missing including the one for 1924. However, in his diary of 1925 Alan is still at Queens School and having a great time. Jack appears to be working at home (Portman and Conquest) and their Uncle Charles is spending a lot of time at East Lydeard.

> **The Devons Lose a Good Man (April 1926).** *Through the death of Mr Charles Morris, Highfield Hall, St. Albans, and Bishop's Lydeard, Somerset, the Devon Cattle Breeders' Society loses one of its best members, and the Red Rubies one their staunchest supporters. In fact it was he that revived the breed from its at one time moribund condition. purchased the best, and what he did not purchase bred, kept them, and exhibited them, and, furthermore, he catered for the interest of the breed overseas, especially in South Africa. But of late years his energies were sapped by continuous ill-health. The name of Charles Morris will be associated with the Devons so long as it remains a breed. He was one those men who were deservedly respected wherever they went.*[18]

---

18 - Western Daily Press – Thursday 8 April 1926

Alan and Jack were both at home on 28 March, 1926, the day that Charles dies at Highfield, and the two brothers go with Amy to St Albans for his funeral on 31 March. Somewhere in the archives there will be a more encompassing obituary for Charles, he had really lived a life of his time, with big highs and lows. A profitable period spent in India when it was a booming colony, before becoming a highly respected farmer in England. He upheld traditions, there was a Highfield Hall cricket team and the estate also hosted annual horse races. He generously gave to local charities both in Highfield and Bishops Lydeard and his will, worth the equivalent of millions of pounds in 1926, changed a large number of lives very significantly.

Even the youngest, most junior farm worker, was given the capacity to try something new. Mr Glanfield, in 1926 and for many years previously, the farm manager of East Lydeard, inherited a sum large enough to start a dairy in Bishops Lydeard.

Almost all Charles's surviving nieces and nephews on the Morris side of the family inherited serious amounts of money. But most significantly, and probably a sign of how close Charles had been to his brother Jack and his young family, our grandfather Jack inherited East Lydeard Farm at the age of 17.

Alan, our great-uncle, inherited more money than many of his cousins. According to Alan's 1926 diary he did not go back to school (which was probably a disappointment to him and certainly a shock to his classmates). He started working on the family farm, Portman.

In 1926 Jack is at Cannington and commuting on a motorbike, which catches fire in May that year. Amy buys the first family car the month after the funeral, she has a few lessons and seems to give it up so Alan drove her around for the rest of her life.

Jack stays at Cannington but the last entry in the diary for 1926 is 27 May…it's likely Jack finished college once probate went through and moved to East Lydeard and Charles's herd of Devon cattle went under the hammer. The next diary we have of Alan's is 1931.

Jack (John Barrington) Morris married Lily (Judy) Tomlinson in Liverpool in 1935. They met because Judy, who had grown up in Lancashire, was teaching at Cannington College…

(Oct 1935). *A popular young member of the Taunton Farmers' Union and the Taunton Vale Harriers' Committee Mr J. B. Morris, was married on Thursday at St Anne's Church, Rainhill, Liverpool to Miss Lily Tomlinson youngest daughter of Mr and Mrs T H Tomlinson of Rainhill, Liverpool. The bridegroom is the eldest son of the late Mr J Morris, and of Mrs Morris of Conquest, Norton Fitzwarren. He took over and occupied East Lydeard in Bishops Lydeard after the death of his uncle the late Mr Charles Morris of Highfield Hall, St Albans the noted breeder of Devon pedigree cattle. The bride, who is also well-known in West Somerset agricultural circles, has for some time been on the staff of the County Farm Institute as an instructress in Dairying. She was given away by her father, and attended by her sister (Miss Lucy Tomlinson). Mr Alan Morris (brother of the bridegroom) acted 'best man'. The honeymoon is being spent on motor tour in Scotland*[19].

Judy (Lily) died of cancer in Musgrove Hospital in 1968.

---

19 - Taunton Courier and Western Advertiser – October 1935

Bishops Lydeard in mourning for funeral of Mrs. Judy Morris (May 1968). Bishops Lydeard and its parish church have suffered a loss by the death of Mrs Judy Morris, wife of Mr Jack Morris, of East Lydeard Farm. She was 59 and died in Musgrove Hospital on 16th May.

Before her marriage to Mr Jack Morris in 1935 she was on the staff of the Cannington Farm Institute where her main subject was flower arranging. A regular worshipper at the local parish church she had been in charge of the floral arrangements there for many years. She was a member of the Committee of the Mother's Union and was a former secretary.

The village was in mourning for the funeral service at the parish church of St Mary's the Virgin, on Monday, conducted by the Rev. Basil St. C.A. Maltin (Vicar). At the organ was Mr Skinner and after the service a muffled peal of bells was rung in her memory.

Family mourners were: Mr J. Morris (husband): Mr and Mrs. Fox (son-in-law and daughter): Mr and Mrs J Morris (son and daughter-in-law): Helen Morris,

Frances Morris, Tom Morris (daughters and son): Mr and Mrs Rebbeck (brother-in-law and sister); Miss Tomlinson (sister); Frank Tomlinson (brother): Mr and Mrs A Morris (brother-in-law and sister-in-law: Mr Graham Skinner (cousin). Mr and Mrs McLoughlin (son-in-law and daughter) were unable to attend.[20]

John Barrington Morris died in 1973.

---

20 - Somerset Gazette – May 1968

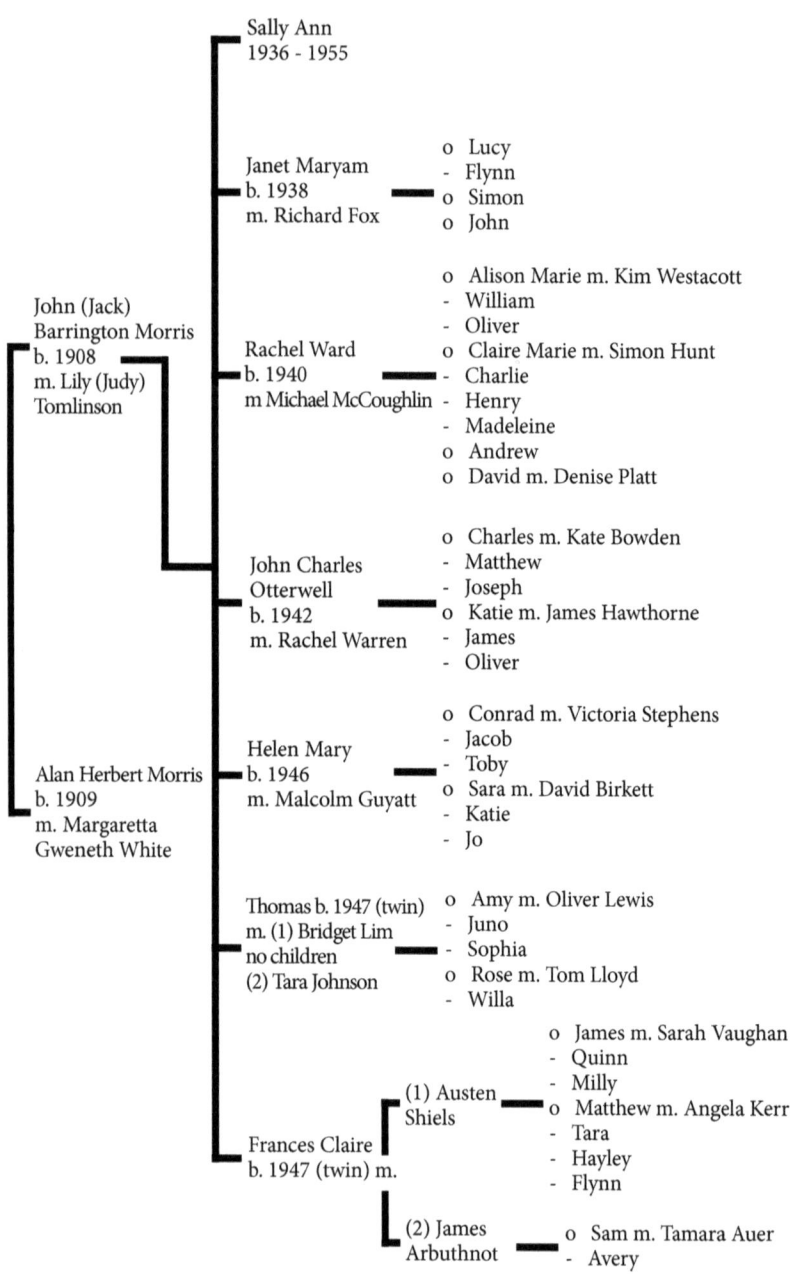

The seven children of John and Lily (Judy) Morris:

Sally Ann Morris
(29 July 1936 – 23 December 1955 after falling from her horse while out hunting)

Janet Maryan Morris/Fox	
Born 16 Feb 1938	
Married Richard Peter Rutherford Fox. They started Foxes Farm Services and were contractors. They had three children.	
Lucy Ann Fox,	Born in Perth, Western Australia. She became a journalist based in Sydney, Nicosia, Moscow and London and travelled the world. She moved to Tasmania in 2003. She has a son Flynn (Evans)
Simon George Fox,	Born at Paradise in Cothelstone and took over the contracting business
John Charles Rutherford Fox	Also born in Cothelstone was a farm manager near Reading and died in his early 40's of MS in Taunton

(Janet) – I think we all had a very happy childhood but as we are all different we all remember things very differently so nobody is right or wrong, we just each have our own memories which make us all different. We have all been very lucky and have coped well with everything that has been thrown at us, which has a lot to do with our upbringing. So all keep well, we have a few more years yet!

Rachel Ward Morris/McLoughlin	
Born 31 Oct 1940	
Married Michael McLoughlin and travelled the world with The Foreign and Commonwealth Office. They had 4 children – Alison, Claire, Andrew and David.	
Alison Marie Mcloughlin/ Westcott	Born in West Berlin in 1965. She travelled the world with her parents before going to boarding school in Shaftesbury. As unaccompanied minors she, Claire, Andrew and David flew each school holiday to join their parents – in Zambia, Bolivia, Mallorca and Ecuador. Half terms were spent with the Fox family in Somerset- often doing the rounds visiting relatives at East Lydeard, Pound, Edgeborough and Bishops Lydeard. Having studied Agriculture she worked for an agricultural supplier and advisory company where she met her husband Kim Westcott (an agronomist). They live in Northamptonshire and have two boys; William studied Engineering and is currently living in Melbourne, Australia working for a motorsport company, Oliver is training in coach building and fabrication for a UK motorsport company.

Claire Marie McLoughlin/Hunt	Born in Iceland in 1967 and married Simon Hunt in Somerset in 1991. She trained as a Nurse in London then moved to Oxford. For the past 10 years she has been working as an Advanced Nurse Practitioner specialising in paediatrics. She and Simon have three children Charlie – working in IT who has a daughter. Henry working in Recruitment, and Madeleine who's just completed Uni, graduating in criminology and Sociology.
Andrew John McLoughlin	Was born in 1970 in Madras India. After travelling a lot in his childhood to the places his parents were posted to, he has settled in Oxfordshire to be close to family and friends. He has made his career in hospitality.
David James McLoughlin	Was an officer in the merchant navy when he met Denise Anne Platt (a buyer in the furniture industry) in Antigua while on holiday during Christmas 1998. They were engaged in Paris in 1999 and married in July 2000 in North Yorkshire. They bought a house in Shiptonthorpe York then moved several times before finally settling in Leavening. David worked as a Humber pilot (navigating vessels along the Humber Estuary) until his health sadly declined in 2011. After a long, brave battle with MS he died in September 2021 aged 47.

(Rachel) – I think we had a very privileged upbringing in many ways, mainly because we were left to our own devises and were completely unaware of what was happening in the outside world. I think that is what Uncle Alan must have meant when he apparently called us 'feral'. How lucky we were to be able to ride out and on to the hills without a second thought – I remember a couple of times having to catch a pony, possibly Trigger, who had dumped me somewhere, but never reporting it when I got back. Uncle Alan occasionally invited two of us to go to the sea (how were we chosen?), with Grandma in hat and longish coat. Who has got the photo of Daddy, Uncle Alan, in jackets and ties, Grandma and one or two of us on a pebbly beach?

Mummy produced two cooked meals a day, Eddy brought in lots of veg from the garden, to my shame I don't remember ever having to help very much in the house. One memory sticks, John and me on the kitchen steps shelling peas but trying to see how far we could shoot them out of the pods, not very helpful! We had some very strange live-in helpers from Tone Vale, Douglas? Rosie (whose mattress was airing almost every day), Weedy, the only ones I can name; more hinderances than helpers I suspect.

What a difference from present day, health-and-safety-bound lives. (Rachel Morris/McLoughlin, March 2023)

John Charles Otterwell Morris	
Born 1942	
Married Rachel Warren and they have farmed Edgeborough, Portman and Pound farms. They have two children – Charles and Katie. John agrees with Francie that the poplar trees at East Lydeard Farm were planted for each of them.	
Charles Morris	Grew up at Edgeborough Farm. He married Kate Bowden in 1992. They have two sons. Matthew Charles Bowden Morris was born in 1995 and is a site supervisor for a fire protection company travelling all over the UK. Joseph William Morris was born in 1998 and after a couple of years working on a sheep farm in New Zealand came back to farm on Edgeborough and run his hog roast business.
Katie Morris/ Hawthorne	Loved growing up at Edgeborough farm with her parents (John and Rachel Morris) and her brother Charlie. My memories are mostly being outside with my pony and a dog or two in tow. She married James Hawthorne in 1998 and they live at Pound Farm, Bishops Lydeard and have two sons, Thomas, 25 and Oliver 23. Thomas is a qualified PE teacher living and working in Melbourne, Australia. Oliver is farming in New Zealand and planning to return home in 2025 to farm at Pound.

Helen Mary Morris/Guyatt	
Born in 1946	
Married Malcolm John Guyatt and had two children. Helen moved to the Lake District in the early 1970's and in 2024 remains living there amongst the beautiful scenery she loves.	
Conrad Morris Guyatt	Born in Whitehaven in 1976 and grew up in the Lake District. He is a Project Manager working in the offshore renewable energy industry installing and burying cables on the ocean seabed. He married Victoria Claire Stephens (also born in 1976 who owns a law practice). They have two children, Jacob and Toby and live in the Northeast of England near Middlesbrough.
Sara Guyatt/ Birkett	Was born in Whitehaven in 1979 and grew up in the Lake District. After living in Aberdeen, Scotland she returned to the Lake District to work as a police officer living in a coastal village close to her mother. She married David Irving Birkett and they have two children – Katie and Jo.

(Helen) – Regarding growing up. A care free time. Riding on the hills, going to pony club rallies and to a week-long camp, girls sleeping in a barn and boys in tents, though we did meet up in the maize at night!

Playing tennis tournaments at Burnham and Sidmouth. I used to ride with Uncle Alan after church and he took me to Wimbledon on the train.

Thomas William Morris (twin of Frances)	
Born July 1949 Married Bridget Limm and then Tara Johnson with whom he has two daughters – Amy and Rose	
Amy Morris/ Lewis	Born in 1987 and raised at East Lydeard. She worked in geographical information systems (GIS/Mapping). She married Oliver Lewis in 2016 and lived and worked in London and San Francisco before moving back to East Lydeard Farm in 2019. In 2024 they are living at Burge Cottage (a cottage on East Lydeard) with their two daughters Juno and Sophia.
Rose Morris/ Lloyd	Born and raised at East Lydeard. She currently lives with her husband Tom Lloyd (who is in sports marketing) and daughter Willa in Stockbridge, Hampshire. In 2024 she went back to work after maternity leave and runs the customer service department for women's fashion company, Wyse.

Frances Claire Morris/Shiels/Arbuthnot (twin of Thomas)

Born July 1949.

Married first Austen Shiels and then James Arbuthnot, she has three sons. Francie moved to Australia in 1970 as a 10 pound pom and in 2024 is living in Ballina on the NSW North coast.

James Shiels	Is a Project Manager specialising in sea floor drilling and soil sampling for geotechnical purposes. His partner is Sarah Vaughan and they have 2 children Quinn and Milly. They live in Ballina, NSW.
Matthew Shiels	Was born in Armidale in 1975 and grew up in Western Sydney. He married Angela Kerr and has three children Tara, Hayli and Flynn. Very entrepreneurial they have lived in many places. He loves the outdoors and mountain bikes, swims, sails, surfs and competes in triathlons. Outback travelling has been a big part of their lives and currently they're on the Gold Coast.
Sam Arbuthnot	Born and raised in Western Sydney and moved to Brisbane to grow the family transport business (Snapes). His partner is Tamara Auer and they have a son Avery and live in Ballina as well.

I(Frances) feel being the youngest my memories are different from others; one regarding the poplar trees in front of the house, I thought I was told seven were planted for each child and a coin put under each one and I often wondered which end was mine!

After Grandma died I spent time with Uncle Alan cleaning and making him his dinner, this particular day he said he was having someone for dinner and could I leave something for him to warm up, so a beef stroganoff was prepared and table set, he then swore me to secrecy saying Margret was his guest and he was going to ask her to marry him, the next day my question being WELL? and with the biggest smile nodded .

My childhood was simple, uncomplicated and a large amount of freedom perhaps that's where the term feral comes in. School was tolerated at Weirfield in Taunton but East Lydeard allowed me to be independent and learn to entertain myself riding being my greatest love with no boundaries. For many years I slept for 3-4 months in the summer house beside the stables, I can still smell the honeysuckle.

I left England when I was 21 and emigrated to Sydney, Australia and at 74 now live in the Northern Rivers NSW an hour away from the Queensland border surrounded by the family husband Jim and 3 sons James, Matthew and Sam plus 6 grandchildren (Tara, Hayley, Flynn, Quinn, Milly and Avery).

I still ride, play golf and enjoy working in my large garden , so that's me in a nutshell what a blessed life . (Francie March 2023).

And now we circle back to where this history started with Alan Herbert Morris.

He left many diaries of his life starting when he was a teenager and going through to the beginning of WWII in 1939 – they are full of life. He worked hard as a farmer at Conquest and Portman, he played cricket and rugby, went to the movies almost every week and loved to bathe (as he called it) whenever he went to a beach. He was very social – his best friends all his life were Ted Gange and Chris Norman and he spent a lot of time visiting cousins and aunts and uncles – he was the great link in the chain between the previous generation of his nine uncles, aunts and many cousins and us.

In around 1950 – he sold Conquest and bought Pound Farm from his cousin Gordon Skinner who retired from farming.

Amy Barrington Morris, his mother, lived with Alan at Pound Farm until she died on 26 April 1967.

He eventually married, in October 1967, when he was 58. Margaretta Gweneth White (Great-Aunt Margaret) was a nursing sister; they had no children.

East Lydeard Farm and Portman Farm remain in the family with brothers Thomas William Morris (East Lydeard) and John Charles Otterwell Morris (Portman) and their families retaining ownership.

Pound Farm is jointly owned by the children of John Charles Otterwell Morris, Charles and Kate Morris and his sister Katie and her husband James Hawthorn and their families.

Copyright 2025 Lucy Fox

lucyfox@bigpond.com

Please contact me if you want more information about anyone mentioned in this history (I have lots more information about everyone) or transcriptions of Alan's diaries.

www.ingramcontent.com/pod-product-compliance
Lightning Source LLC
LaVergne TN
LVHW050141080526
838202LV00062B/6545